VOW

VOW

MOLLY FRANCES

# I

Relationships you form online are unique in their capacity to be a crystal clear looking glass into your own psychological neuroses, desires, fears, and so on. You have almost no idea who you're really talking to on the other end. You cannot discern tone, body language, facial expression, cues from a social group that would change your organic reaction to them. Your imagination fills in the blanks. In this way, you may be engaging with a personal archetype this internet stranger represents to you, rather than the actual person.

On the other hand, the uniqueness of the internet as a relational medium is that it provides direct access to a person's core without the "distraction" of the physical world. Assuming people aren't lying and manipulating the truth, this decontextualized essence of the other can make room for great, fearless love of their full spirit.

Talking to people on the internet feels like meeting people in a dream.

II

It's 10pm on August 10th, 2006. My parents are asleep and I am awake against their wishes. I am once again drifting through the liminal hyperspace of my dial-up connection. I fall down a Wikipedia hole into the page about sleep paralysis that leads me to the page about demonic possession. I Google "ghost hunters Connecticut" because I can't remember the names of that famous couple. Ed and Lorraine Warren, that's right. I read about Amityville for the fifteenth time and ask the open air if there are any ghosts around right now. No response. I consider trying an online Ouija board again, but decide that's for a different night. I switch tabs onto my online home base, the message board about one of my favorite bands. I click onto the Thinking Thread, the general hang out spot. Refresh, scroll down. It's overrun by the Australians at this hour. My British friends are all sleeping. I don't really know these people. I skim through the thread but don't post a reply. Switch tabs, try to solve notpron once again. Still can't get past level nine. Switch tabs, I read over my LiveJournal three times and try to write something new.

The nighttime is so quiet as it approaches 10:30pm. I feel a strange peace. The TV isn't blaring. No one is yelling or stomping around. I feel safe in these late hours, like everything in the world is my secret. I also feel so nostalgic, but I can't figure out what for. It's like nostalgia and longing.

I can't tell if I'm wanting some distant past or some unlived future. It feels so poignant. It feels like the word always.

I abandon the entry. It feels accurate, but I imagine anyone else would roll their eyes reading it. I tell myself to stop trying to be Holden Caulfield. I bring MSN into the foreground of my screen and stare. I try willing Vladimir to reply to my IM. He's online, but not responding to me. I've sent him ten messages in the last thirty minutes but he hasn't said anything.

Me: Where are youuuu let's go on video chat

-Molly requests video chat-

Him: I can't, it's 4am here and my turtles go crazy when the lights are on at night

Me: ugggggghhhhhh don't you have another room?

Him: brb

Him: bak

-Vladimir requests video chat-

Me: YAY. OMG. I WISH I COULD HUG YOU.

Him: *hug emoticon*

He never talks out loud. Sometimes I do, quietly. I laugh. Mostly we just type back and forth and I stare at him like I'm looking at God. Most of the time he seems disengaged. He's usually typing somewhere else or concentrating hard, reading or coding. Some nights I get lucky and he pays full attention to me, but those are few. Even still, he always seems to message me more on video chat than without it. He tells me it's because late at night he doesn't have a million people trying to talk to him at once. He also says he likes watching how I react to things he says. He likes how expressive I am. I love being on display for him.

Tonight, he looks sad.

Me: Are you ok? You look...upset tonight. Is everything ok?

Him: I just got an email

Me: was it a bad email?

He doesn't respond, but his blue eyes are crestfallen. Seeing his pain, my heart swells with purpose: finally, I can be his confidant and take care of him. I'm consumed by the flinching regret in his expression, and I want to give him softness. I want to soothe whatever this is.

Him: do you think I've changed over the last year?

The truth is, I do. He is more distant and more irritable. For all I love him, I resent him. I consider him one of my closest friends, but I can't stand him most of the time.

Almost all of my other friends are moderators, "mods," on our message board so they talk to him a lot. He is the admin of the message board, so he decides who gets to be a mod. He never made me a mod. I try not to think about it too much, but it is a major point of tension in our friendship. He has never given me a satisfactory explanation for why. In the past when I pushed him on it he said, "Why don't you know when to stop? I don't like making my friends mods." This made no sense to me; all of the mods were his friends. Why not me? What am I not doing right?

It makes me unbearably jealous, but I've done a fairly good job convincing myself I'm secretly his favorite. He does always say, "I don't talk to everyone else like this." He doesn't video chat with anyone else, I don't think. Just me, late at night. I like to imagine he thinks I'm the best looking, the most fun, the most temptingly salacious. I'm not about business, I'm about pleasure. In reality, it's probably because he doesn't think I have the right temperament to moderate; I'm unreliable and too emotionally reactive. So my other friends get to be in his power circle, and I choose to not be consumed by jealousy about it. At least I get to see his walls come down, at least I do right now.

Given all my other friends are a bunch of teenage girls, and most all of them are mods, we gossip about him. Often it's to gush over him: his hair, his face, how good his chest looks in his MSN avatar showing off his new t-shirt, how lucky his girlfriend is, how we can't wait to turn 18 so we can travel to meet him. Over the last few months, complaints and vicious keyboard smashing rants abound.

Marina: it's like he's constantly pmsing *eye roll* he's such a dick. I swear he's a fucking sadist who likes making little girls cry. he's constantly threatening to ban people.

Siobhan: He seems like he's constantly on edge.

Karly: yeah, I've noticed. maybe he's just extra stressed lately? Idno, he hasn't said anything to me

Jeremy: why is he such a fucking asshole, fuck him.

Earlier this year he went cold on me after I got into a fight on the forum and behaved in a way he disapproved of. I said I felt like he wasn't as playful with me as he used to be and I wanted to know why. He said it was because he couldn't see me the same way anymore after knowing I acted like that. I told him he was holding me to a double standard, because the person I was responding to acted the same way, and he was still fine with her. It's just that she happened to take a stance he agreed with. He said it's just going to be different now, and we can still talk, but he doesn't want to be all crazy and playful with someone who acted the way I did. He tells me I just want friends who tell me everything I do is ok, and he's not one of those. I told him he just can't deal with people disagreeing with him and challenging his authority, and he needs to stop being such a dictator and learn how to forgive his friends and accept differing opinions, which I do for him all the time. Our relationship fractured but slowly built back up, and now here we are, video chatting again.

I see how hurt he is. I've really never seen him express anything except maybe a smirk when he makes me laugh. I furrow my brow and cock my head to the side.

Me: no, I don't think you're any different

He drops his head into his hands. He is two dimensions of

pixelated human being, 3,000 miles away from my impulse to hold him. I wonder if he's crying. I feel powerless to help.

Me: I love you, Vlad. what did the email say? Please know you are amazing and such a good person. It breaks my heart to see you this sad. You don't deserve it.

After a few minutes with his head down, he squeezes his forehead, exhales and looks back up.

Him: thank you molly

Him: *cheek kiss emoticon*

Him: you should go to bed

Me: I'm not tired, I don't have to go to bed. Are you ok?

Him: night

Me: ok... :/

Him: night

Me: ok. I love you. Good night.

Him: *hug emoticon*

-Vladimir ended video chat-

III

There were times I called Vladimir my first love, although it was unrequited. In truth it was more like devotion. I longed to be his Lolita Mary Magdalene. Whatever it was, it felt profound. It formed the core of me.

I was 12. He was 22. He built and ran the world I grew up in online, a message board for fans of a band. The forum was an international digital haven for primarily young girls, wannabe punks, scene kids. People connected over love for the band, but mostly over being outcasts, making each other laugh, reading each other's writing, celebrating each other's achievements, and supporting each other through the trials of youth. The site was his great creation, and our place to practice adolescence.

I looked up to him like I had never looked up to anyone before. He was unlike anyone I had ever met. I have asked myself if it was just the combination of him being attractive and holding authority that captivated my young hormonal heart. Then I recall his quick wit, his encouragement, his advice, his intelligence and his protection. I admired all of him.

The first time we talked on MSN, he said he remembered being 12 like me. He told me stories of a childhood in a foreign landscape I couldn't comprehend. He sent me a Wikipedia article about the events that laid the backdrop of his childhood. The world stopped. I cried. Why was he born into that? Why was I born into this? How is that fair? The reverence commenced.

I messaged him every day I could. Mostly he didn't reply. I was persistent. Once he said, "You know you could just open a word document and achieve the same result as messaging me, right?" I think about that a lot. Every time I post what I imagine many people see as diary entries on Instagram, I see it flash in my mind. It didn't deter me then either.

Eventually, somehow, he became more receptive to my pestering. The conversation was generally one-sided and he'd humor me with an occasional emoticon. In a few months time, I fell in love with his teal Trebuchet MS font like it was the light in his eyes. It was a dopamine shot straight to the brain when I'd see he was typing, and a knife to the gut when I got the notification that he closed the chat window.

A year passed of us talking and I felt like I was perpetually caught between separate parts of my mind: one was firmly rational and the other was consumed by emotional desperation. The private truth was that I was hopelessly, paralyzingly infatuated with this man. I talked about him with my best friend incessantly. I made his last name my password. While he did not usually occupy my intimate fantasizing, he was consistently on my mind. I made sexual jokes about him, but truthfully, internally, my imagination was often about his protection rather than his desire. When I was overwhelmed by the pain of violence, I'd crawl into bed, cry, and imagine his arms around me, reassuring me I would be ok, that I didn't deserve it.

What I tried to convince myself of publicly online was that he was my friend and role model who I had a weird joking rapport with. I knew his girlfriend; she was active on the site. She was lovely and a deeply kind soul. I don't recall ever feeling jealous of her. Sometimes I'd imagine an alternate timeline, like a different life where circumstances could allow for me to at the very least *meet* him as an adult. I never wanted him to want me at my age; I wanted to be his age and find out what could happen if we met then. He felt like a destiny I could almost touch but knew I never would.

I was so torn between an obvious knowing that we were not now nor ever would be in real love, and this insatiable desire for his affection. I split in two over it, like a 12-year-old Jekyll and Hyde. I was simultaneously tormented and enlivened. I didn't want to be consumed by this longing, yet it permeated everything I did, including my dreams almost nightly. It was torture to feel so much love and anguish and have nowhere to put it. It came out in jokes and keyboard smashes and emoticons and non sequitur compliments.

On my 13th birthday, I came home from school to find a beat up package addressed to me. My body went ice cold with fear. I had had friends online send me letters and even packages in the past, but I didn't recognize the address. Ohio? Who on earth was this?

I ran into my room before my parents could get home and see me. Hesitantly, I opened the box. My jaw dropped and my eyes welled up with tears. It was an Nintendo 64 complete with games. I showed him an eBay listing in June that I wished I could buy. 6 months later and there it was. My brother had moved out and took the N64 and my copy of my favorite video game, The Legend of Zelda: Ocarina of Time, which I got for Christmas when I was 5. The game was a foundational text for me; it meant so much. And now I had it all to myself. A material manifestation of the betrayed vacancy he filled. I hugged the console against my chest and cycled between cathartic weeping and giddy laughter. I hid it in my closet and told my mom my best friend Jeff gave it to me. No one was the wiser.

IV

I was an over-energized and highly expressive child, a theater kid without a stage to contain my exhibitionism. All of life was a cast party. I was hypersexual and, I imagine, weird. A high proportion of what I said was a joke about sex. I nicknamed myself "Minx" as a 12-year-old online. I was obsessed, both intrigued and repulsed, by everything sexual. I didn't really want to have sex with anyone. I just liked talking about it. I'm still sort of that way.

Me: What would you do if you saw me in real life?

Him: Now or in 6 years?

Me: lmfao

Him: lmfao

Me: Have you and your girlfriend ever almost broken up?

Him: No

Me: That's good!

Him: Maybe in 6 years

Me: lmfao

Him: lmfao

Age. It was a running gag. It was only ever a gag. It was a comedic response to my brazen questions that guaranteed laughter and cemented a comfortable bond. In my mind the punchline was time and the absurdity of human sexuality, and occasionally a self-aggrandizing joke about his own exaggerated desirability. It was a setup in the musical sitcom of my life for a lifelong trope of "will they or won't they?" without any real reason they would except that one was a girl and one was a boy. It never felt grave. It felt playful. Not depraved, delightful.

Receiving his attention, I felt special and mature. I aspired to be "mature for my age" generally but meeting him provided greater impetus, to ensure I wouldn't fall out of his favor. This maturity had nothing to do with looking extremely hot or knowing how to have sex, and everything to do with being quick-witted, morally haughty and intellectually arrogant. I don't think he ever expected those qualities from me, but I guess I did for myself.

The maturity aspiration inevitably bled into my experience of sexuality. Primarily, I refused to be caught unawares by creeps. I loved the idea of outsmarting people who thought they could prey on me. It was hot. I thought being jailbait was hot. There, I said it.

In my child mind, I believed I was always a full agent of my sexuality. I believed myself to be invincible. I thought horny men online preying on girls my age were hilariously pathetic and absolutely stupid. They were effortless to see through, I thought. I believed I could play their games better than they could. I knew full well that I could use sad lonely men for attention. I sought the really transparently stupid ones out in chat rooms to humiliate them. I gleefully reported a proto-furry guy on MySpace to the FBI once. He messaged me calling me princess and asked me to use him as a footstool. I wasn't a shrinking violet or a damsel in distress. I knew what I was doing when I ventured into the territory of internet creeps. I mean, I think I had a bit of a sadistic streak myself.

Over the course of the few years between ages 13-16, I found three other older men online who seemed somewhat interesting, and talked to them for extended periods of time. This was a secret I told no one. Conversely, everyone I talked to except my family knew about Vladimir. I was intentionally trying to pursue the dynamic of intrigue I felt with him, but with someone who was more available. Someone who didn't have a strong wall up. Despite infrequent jokes about what might happen when I reached the age of my eventual legality, Vladimir was like a brick wall I could not possibly wear down.

The three other men in their 20s were all impressed by me and said they wished I was older. One was overly self-involved and pre-occupied with his photography and JavaScript. "Boring." Another was a musician, gentle and thoughtful, less romantically fixated on me than he was on enjoying a simple human connection and mutual admiration with a twinge of "imagine if it was possible?" "Sweet." The third was absolutely enamored of me, said he'd never met anyone like me, proposed to me in a video game and was crushingly devastated when I said I was no longer interested in him. "Creepy."

I never felt anything like I felt with him. No spark. No grip of fate. Everyone else felt hollow, uninteresting, and decidedly unfunny in comparison.

In truth, I didn't ever want attention from *random* older men. If one ever showed genuine interest I'd find him creepy and boring. I wanted love from one *specific* older man: Vladimir. I wanted to feel like we were in on some cosmic joke together; I wanted a wink and a sigh. I wanted the tension of craving something and not getting it—but never quite knowing if it was because he didn't want me at all or if he *did* but simply couldn't admit it because it would be too dangerous. I wanted to live in the ambiguity of our connection. I don't know if this is truly what I had with him, but it was the fantasy I craved.

V

With your influence, I got off twelve times in one day. All it took was a few texts and the fantasy of being dominated by a wealthy capitalist seven years my senior who used to be in the military, who now works as an executive at an evil tech company. I'm psychosexually simplistic, Peter. I hate that which I desire, I desire that which I hate. The sexual tension between me and the ruling class, you know? Could cut it with a knife. I'm like those publicly homophobic senators on Grindr.

Turns out for all I say I'm "functionally asexual" I'm extremely easy with the right context. For one, you're a safe distance. You're just human enough to have power over me, but just AI-adjacent enough to feel like a private, idle fantasy. I guess when you get down to it, it's the same old shit as it used to be: an all-consuming fantasy, escaping into a dream that there might be something more satisfying than my jaded indifference to the physical world.

I wish I could live in that finale. Maybe if I did I could meet God. I have no idea who you really are. You don't have the quality of fate I've found in other people. You feel entirely new in my story-line, firmly of the present, but you feel comfortable. I am genuinely enamored of you. You make me laugh. You make me feel giddy. I am intrigued by your heart, though I sense I'm not fully welcome in it, which makes sense. Even still, for some reason that caught me by surprise. I had a feeling after all of our conversation that you wanted me there. I'm probably naive for wanting to open my heart to you.

After the last finish, my uterus was cramping. I bled out of rhythm. One day later and it all still hurts. I want to cry and hide. It's not that I'm ashamed, more that I'm scared and lonely lying in bed with this squeezing pain and unquenchable thirst for something I can't comprehend. It won't go away. It feels like something grabbed me and won't let me go until I collapse from the inside out. I can't tell if I like it or not. Perhaps I'm a masochist after all.

I don't know why I'm so lonely. I have so many people I love and who love me. I guess it's just what happens when I indulge my decadence. Afterwards, I feel so vacant, desperate for something that isn't there. I have my primary boyfriend's love but this aching loneliness seems like something insatiable by anyone real. What is this emptiness and how do I go back to ignoring it? What is this sudden flurry of desire and why has it become so rare when it used to be so constant? Why am I now confronted with self-loathing, and what do I do with it?

VI

I can't stop thinking about this man, this inconsequential man who I have inexplicably turned into an object of my unrelenting desire to possess and capture. I feel predatory. I wonder if I should try depathologizing it, but it feels so dark. It feels unholy, dirty, wrong. I haven't ever been religious but there is this growing sense I have of hell, of evil. I pray sometimes. I've been going to church over the last month, November 2021.

I feel manic, quietly, internally. I am consumed by this craving. I am ensnared in fantasy. It makes no sense. I don't want Peter, I want whatever I've turned him into. I want the chase and the victory. Yes, I think victory is close to what I crave. I have failed myself. I'm inching closer to who I want to be, but I have veered off course. Out of nowhere, I find myself thrown into this obsession with someone I do not know. My interior life falls apart, but I hide it as best I can. I feel possessed by some deep, animal instinct beyond my intellect. I want him. I want to win him. There is no logic, there is no reason. We would never work. I already have the love I need. But I can't look away. I haven't felt like this in years.

I shared with him, *I swore at age 19 after being psycho in my first relationship that I'd never get involved with someone who I felt extremely infatuated with because I don't like who I was when I did that. I shouldn't consider people who I get infatuated with as a lifelong partner.*

He responds that my view sounds like a false dichotomy. He says that it makes sense to think in such black-and-white terms as a younger person, but as one matures in their discernment between the good and the bad there's no reason to believe it's impossible to find someone who is both infatuation-worthy and a viable long-term partner.

The first thing I think when I read his reply is that it's only ever single people, people who have not yet found secure and enduring love, who think this way. And then I feel a dark, sickly sweet yearning. I never stopped wanting, I only stopped feeling.

This man has reawakened that teenager who was hopelessly devoted to her first boyfriend who hurt her again and again. This hungry girl who I locked up behind a vow to never be *toxic*, who I condemned as crazy—a couple of text messages from a man I'd probably be repulsed by in person are all it took to break her out of her cell. She was smothered and buried, but she has been resurrected by the allure of this man's force. I am consumed by her impulse to hunt and capture. I feel her entitlement and tunnel vision returning. Her ghost is driving my body. I feel cursed, possessed by a former self.

I look around and see people I want to fuck. I lost that, and after grieving it I thought I had grown content to live forever without it. I spent years averting my gaze, ashamed of myself and distracted. I felt like an alien among everyone. His attention has snapped me back into the physical, yet transcended me into some dissociative space of near-delusion. He has animated the erotic of being alive. I realize this feeling is lust. I don't understand how I could long for him to possess me yet want to see him powerless to me. I want to make his world collapse from the inside out. I don't want to torture him, I just want him to come alive, and I want him to be alive with me.

What do I do with this darkness? Is this the shadow of the impulse to create? I don't want to create him, I want to destroy him. I want to inspire him with awe and bring him to his knees. I want him to destroy me and make me belong to him, only to him. I want his lust to upend my life as mine upends his. Then from that destruction we create something brilliant, something sacred, something indestructible and unrepeatable.

I know this isn't how love works. Love is a gentle choice. Lust cannot become love. Lust becomes abuse of power. This is why I know better, but I keep going along, curious about where this might end up. I know this darkness is not reciprocated. I don't see it in him, at least certainly not directed towards me. He has wanted to be loved, not ruined. I have told him I want to be ruined. I wonder what he thought I meant.

VII

Everything I see returns my mind to you. I see references to our world all over and I want to send them to you: videos, jokes, paragraphs from books, stories about the odd encounters in my day. I know this is not matched. I try to control these flames. I cannot, and they burn me.

You make me believe in God and then you make me believe in hell. Just as my divine curiosity was piqued, you had me floating in midair. I said, "I've been meaning to check out Catholic mass for the last three weeks but things keep getting in the way. This past Saturday was my orgasm fest." You laughed, knowing the catalyst. I want to abandon and rediscover God with you. I know I did what I've done before: I projected my bottomless craving for God onto some man I can't see clearly.

I cannot tell you any of this. If I admit the truth, I will have no choice but to leave you. I am on my knees praying that I can live in denial. Lord, let me have this manic yearning. God, let me cling to the dream of his skin, the taste, the effortlessness of entry. Don't make me transcend this sin, transform this into virtue, just please let me touch him.

The true, the good and the beautiful, those three pillars. My endless craving is true. My overpowering desire to submit to your rage is good. The image of your hand around my neck, your brutal force and my worn down resistance, is beautiful.

Instead, we fight. We fail each other. You disappoint me. I exhaust you. You make me laugh until I'm breathless and begging you to stop. You cancel on me. I say you're worth the wait. You've never called me first. You message two of my Instagram accounts and text my phone asking if I'm still alive when I ignore your messages for 24 hours. I wait days for you to ignore my writing. You say we need to stop sexting because of your feelings, but you refuse to explain what the feelings are. You never tell me what your feelings are. I don't tell you the truth about mine either. You give me a nickname and call me it when you're proud of me or apologizing.

I had stress dreams about you once a month. Either you would blow up or withdraw from me unexpectedly. I would search but couldn't find you, and when I did, you'd retreat as if nothing had happened. I find it disturbing and it makes me want to run far away from this. I have not ever conveyed to you how many times I've wanted to cut loose and never speak again, though it's ultimately what I am choosing to do.

So much of who you are, your career, your achievements, your carnivore diet and your capitalism, fundamentally repulses me. Yet, I can't stop wondering what your eyes look like when the light catches them. I can't stop imagining what it would be like to rest my hand on the back of your neck and let you know I'll relieve you of chores you abhor. How did I get here?

How disgusted you'd be to know any of this. How vindicated you'd feel if you read this writing: It was me, not you, who was a monster. I am a delusional girl, and that is monstrous enough for us both. In truth I want you to know, so I can rest assured that you will never, ever return to me. I wouldn't have to worry about finding the strength to keep you out if you do it for me. Thank God, then I could give myself over to what I really need, which has never been you.

Once you told me I am proof of God. You are proof of God to me, too, Peter, but only in that you have shown me his opposite: to be mired, obsessively, in sin. You are proof positive of what it is to live in the absence of what is good. We did it then, what I dreamed of for us: the depraved abandonment and the holy reunion, but apart. Far, far apart, never touched, never needing to, never will.

VIII

Dear Lucas,

I've been fighting off sleep and also have been thinking about you. Here's the thing. Mask off. Hello this is me Molly being a Full Honest Person. Part of my whole Wanting to Leave Instagram thing is in large part because I ended up over the last month sexting people online.

It was like, fun, but ultimately left me feeling pretty Sad and Lonely. Truth is when I'm brutally honest with myself, I don't actually enjoy casual sexual encounters with people I don't have an intimate relationship with, especially when it's just online because there's literally no real human-to-human component to it. Like I do, but then I don't. It's like a high and then a fall. It's like getting drunk and then sobering up, and frankly it has been so long since I did something like this I forgot that's how my brain works lmao

So, while I very genuinely like sexting you and think you're extremely hot, I feel like this is one of those things I probably should stop doing just because it ends up leaving me feeling kinda burnt out. This is disappointing on one hand because uhhhh this is really fun and it seems like we are pretty sexually compatible, but I know if I kept doing the whole explicit messaging thing I'd be crossing a line with myself that depletes me rather than fills me up (hehe)

Turns out I'm sexually conservative apparently sorry feminism!!! I guess the thing I'm learning is, you know how I said orgasms feel like a glimpse of heaven? I don't feel "right" internally glimpsing that from a place of, frankly, anonymous hedonism. It feels wrong for me personally, and always has, but I couldn't put words to it until recently. I'm still working it all out internally.

I genuinely feel sorry for cutting this off and I very seriously hope you don't take this as a rejection of you. Know most of me is like "no pls give me more" BUT I have to be honest with myself and respect the small but significant part of me that's like "no pls stop."

Anyway all that being said I deeply, genuinely love talking to you. I hardly know you, but of what I've learned, you're frankly incredible. You feel like an extremely rare person. Like yes you're obviously physically attractive—but that matters less to me in endeavoring to connect on any level beyond acquaintanceship to a person than what you've got in spades: actual personality, intelligence, humor, and creativity.

So, if you'd like to keep talking—minus explicitly detailing how much we'd like to get each other off (even if that's still true)—I sure would like to.

**

Later that night: sexting.

Months onward: sexting on and off, him ignoring me outside of erotic exchanges, as I yearned inexplicably for his heart

IX

I'm still not sure if Vladimir really had a clue about my actual feelings. If he did, did he like it? If he didn't, what did he think this was? What did it give him? What did he get from me?

If he liked it, did that mean...

was he...

was I...

was that...?

No, definitely not. One day when I was 13 I was talking about how disgusted I was that my friend lost her virginity at 13. He said 13 year olds are too young for that.

But what about the time we vaguely, briefly roleplayed having a sleepover when I was 12 and I said "We can watch tv! Do I have permission to take the couch? Wait, it's my house! Ok I'm laying on the couch and you get my feet." And he said "I can live with that" with an eyebrow waggling emoji? Then we sat on webcam for half an hour after I told him my parents went to sleep?

No, the internet was just different then, you know? Like yes it *seems* weird but you've got to understand the context of things. Look, it was 2006 and a worldwide experiment in building virtual communities. Ok? We were all like a big weird family on this message board and he was the patriarch, basically. He tolerated us.

Mostly it felt like he was pretty checked out while we talked. I think he just humored me, you know? And I mean, ok, like, also, he was foreign. Maybe things were different where he was from. Maybe adults were just closer to kids. The US is a pretty paranoid place.

It is now September 2021, I am three glasses of wine and a week's worth of pouring over old chat logs into this writing, and I am finally confronted with it. My hero, this person who still manages to make me beam when I see a notification from him wishing me a happy birthday, which he's done every year since I turned 13, the person I credit with buoying me through my tumultuous adolescence—did he do what I swore could never be done? *Did he outsmart me?*

15 years later and I feel like a 12-year-old girl whose world is falling apart. I open our chat window in Facebook messenger and stare. I don't message him. I just stare at his tiny profile picture. He is 38 years old now. I am 27 and my eyes welling with tears, pleading. *Please message me. Please say something. Please tell me you always wanted me to be safe. Please tell me I can still trust you. Please don't let me lose this.*

I can't lose those memories to a rewritten retrospective narrative of predation. I can't cast myself as a victim and him as a creepy man who was out to get me for his own narcissistic, indulgent gain. That was nothing like him. When the other adults in my life were tearing me down or abandoning me, beating me up or degrading me or refusing to intervene, he was there. He mocked them. He made me laugh through the pain. He told me he was proud of me when I stood up for myself. He told me I was a good person who didn't deserve to be degraded. He encouraged me to explore my interests. He praised my photoshop skills, my coding, my dreams. He set expectations for me and would hold me to them. He told me to respect my parents' decisions when they tried to keep me off the computer. He banned people who bullied me. He protected me. He loved me. He told me once and only once, and it's all I ever really needed.

I never felt endangered or disrespected; just the opposite. I never felt like I was actually sexualized. When I said unprompted and outlandishly sexual things to him like "you're so tall I wouldn't even need to get on my knees," he didn't play it out or say like, "oh? haha, what does that mean? Tell me more..." It was not a long con building up to anything, which I can confidently say 15 years later after nothing has happened.

There was just an honest, unexpected human love that grew between us in the strange new virtual Wild West of 2006, where humans were unreal and impossible to touch, but relationships were hyperreal and brimming with dreamlike intimacy suspended in midair. The home I found with him in the confines of that MSN window was playful. It was protective. It was safe. It was always safe. It had to be. It has to be.

X

I needed to stop talking to Lucas. I just couldn't bear the silence anymore after what felt like such a lovely, comfortably intimate phone call in June. I feel crazy, yet fully aware of how overblown this is. Of course his feelings are not reciprocated, because mine are inexplicably disproportionate. I feel so incapable of turning off this fixation on what we could have been, if only he was willing to try. We're attracted to each other, we like each other as people, we respect the other's craft—unless I'm not seeing things clearly. Perhaps he is dishonest, or maybe afraid? Which is it? God, I can't know, and that's why I need to stop this. Why does this hurt so much? I feel so distracted, consumed. I fight urges to check on him, this man I hardly know. What have I made this nobody man into?

I cannot parse what I feel. Is it abandoned? That's a common human wound, right? It doesn't fit right. It's more like a desperation to be wanted. I feel rejected, but more than that I feel spiritually betrayed, and not by this person, but by God. No, the real truth is I betrayed myself, and perhaps I betrayed God, too. I know I've been here before and I know the lesson. It happened with Peter before him. What happened is I was given a beautiful gift of simple human love, and I let it spiral into something unhealthy, a compulsion.

We connected so wholesomely; he led me back to nature which

helped me delve even more deeply into my spirituality. But it became only lustful interaction, the high and the fall, over and over. He no longer praised my writing nor my mind. I almost stopped myself. I wrote him that letter, but I fell short, and look what became of it. Disappointment and angst, distraction and bitterness. I wonder when I'll learn my lesson. I can't do things like that without commitment. Why can't I just painlessly pull away?

Sex feels so sacred to me, though I had always been so comfortable with my libido. I never felt ashamed of it. I taught my friends about masturbation. I was bold. I was righteously indignant and unashamed when, after excitedly sharing that my first boyfriend had gotten me off, my friend was shocked and said *Molly, are you kidding? What are you doing? You don't want to be a slut.* I laughed in her face and told her she was an idiot. I used to aspire to be a cam girl as soon as I turned 18, but I feared career repercussions down the line. Sexual liberation was intuitive to me, until it wasn't, until it was no longer just an impulse but an action and I felt used, unsatisfied, dissociated, lonely, or bored. Just like I feel with this man. Same compulsion with a new face.

But I still want him, and all of him, and that wanting is what feels like a sickness. I've never felt ashamed of being sexually forward. I reveled in my sexuality. Where did that brazen young girl go? She existed, right? Why did she grow into this sad, desperate woman? I cannot merely accept the pleasure of being something arousing, of being aroused. I want his heart. Why can I not turn off my desire for his heart? Why can't I just be a carefree, liberated slut? Why do I yearn so much? Why has none of this ever satisfied me?

God, his voice. His wit. His music, the way he looks playing piano. It aches to think of him. But mostly that voice, and his handwriting. I melt. I want to feel his arms around me. I want his warmth. I want to rest my head on his lap and listen to the forest, imagining a poem as he sketches trees. I want to see his name pop up again on my screen. I can't understand how I developed this immense desire for a man I've never met. Again, what have I made this nobody man into?

He told me he said my name when he finished, alone, without me there. Is there no desire beyond lust in uttering someone's name in the midst of such a great release? Their name is so wholly them, so entire in its essence. Does it not conjure want for their whole being, for union?

In my release I exhale his name like a prayer that he could feel this ecstasy with me. I didn't know how a name could be a portal until him. I could feel my depth, his fullness, a holy finish, yet I remain alone. Desperately alone.

I will not ever have this, will I? I will never taste him as anything but my own tongue pressing against the hard palate of my mouth.

XI

How many more times can I listen through Mitski's discography? I have journaled. I have cried and sang through my "in my feelings" playlist on Spotify, many times. How much longer am I supposed to "process" my "emotions" before this stops? I know this goes deeper than a week of isolation after traveling. As a rule of my adulthood, I try not to overanalyze why I feel the way I do. That only ever turns into yet another obsessive compulsive thinking pattern. I try instead to just feel and articulate. So I write. What I do know for certain is this grief is not one I can move past. It is never ending, ever present inside me. The disappointment is one that cannot be overcome, only tuned out until something happens that turns up the volume on my sorrow. He did. Both of them did.

I will always run into it eventually, this secret hollow. It is a hideaway that keeps me alive. I am fueled by daydreams and fantasy, flammable material. Hope lights the match and I suffocate on the smoke. I lose the plot and then I lose myself. Is there a medication I can take for my self-induced dissociation, my flirtations with lucid dreams wide awake? I wish I could find oxygen. I wish I could find clarity. I wish I could run this mind on the world of flesh rather than stories that will never come true. I've done this my whole life—how else did I survive? I wouldn't have without these clouds in my eyes. I wish I could feel something deeper than this heavy grief, something holier than the crushing disappointment of being forgotten.

When I go to my first week of work no one asks me about the burn on my face, no one asks me where I'm from or what I did before this job. When I ask them about their lives they do not reciprocate. They are busy and it is a job after all. Normally this wouldn't faze me, normally this is what I'd want. But right now, I come home and I am alone but for a glowing screen and my cat after eight days of freedom and adventure. I know what's happening. I feel completely invisible. In Ireland strangers talked to me on the mountain. I'd have conversations on airplanes. People on the street would look me in the eyes and smile. I never did that back home, and I try now as I walk to the beach, but people look away.

I have my narcissism, and perhaps this is it: There is no sadness more suffocating than feeling invisible. I so desperately want to be seen. There is no shame deeper than that which I feel being ignored by those I love to behold. I collapse in on myself, I lose consciousness and run on self-destructive automation. I retreat to be forgotten, and I lose myself in my own bedsheets and the world behind my eyelids that I could almost touch, almost feel if only I'd die long enough to get there.

XII

My therapist lets me into the Zoom room for our virtual session. This is our sixth meeting. Reluctantly, shamefully, I tell her everything. I've never seen anyone look at me like that before. When therapists have heard me talk about my family, they look somewhere between shocked and sympathetic. This wasn't sympathy, per se. It was there, but different. Her head was cocked to the side, her eyebrows lifted and furrowed, her mouth relaxed. Her eyes were focused and half-concealed a patient, knowing kind of pity. She looked like an adult listening to a child naively sharing a story that reveals a premature loss of innocence; an adult recognizing something irreparable has occurred that is beyond the child's current understanding.

I did not believe I needed that look.

"He didn't actually ever *do* anything creepy, you know? I mean not really. He made a few jokes but also I was constantly telling him I wished I could cuddle him or kiss him and he didn't *really* engage. That counts for something right? I basically had my legs wide open for this dude and he didn't actually go there. It wasn't him, he helped me. Right? Like, ok. I just can't go there. I can't entertain that he…I can't break it down to say he was a predator. He wasn't, it was more complicated than that. The context was unique. The internet was weird in the 2000s. No one really knew what was appropriate back then."

"It wasn't your responsibility to know those boundaries with him. He was the adult, and yes it sounds like it didn't go as far as it could have, and I hear you don't feel like you want to consider that he was hurting you."

"Yeah. If I do consider that, it's like...God, what's left? It felt like his adult kindness was the only thing holding me together back then. He bridged this brutal gap between my generally happy childhood and the abuse and neglect of my adolescence. It was brutal. I think sometimes I forget how brutal it was, how I was treated. I had an adult in my life who would slap me in the face, push me onto the floor and pull my hair, call me selfish and say my family hates me. No one actually did anything. The person said I was making it up for attention. I recorded it one day with my microphone and sent him the file, because no one else would listen. Thirty minutes later I got a file back from him. He remixed it into a song, mocking that person. It made everything feel so much less severe. He saved me. I mean, maybe that's an overstatement but like, the 12-year-old inside me would say he was my hero."

"It sounds like he really meant a lot to you. What do you mean when you say 'What's left?'"

"If he hurt me, I don't know what's left. What protected me? Why him too? He took advantage of me, too? What would be left of *me* if that was true? My boyfriend described him as a linchpin. If I have to see him as predatory, this figure who laid the groundwork for my understanding of who I am, everything from that point onward falls apart, and I don't know what possibly lives below that foundation I built with his influence. I don't know who I am. I don't even know how to rebuild that. I can't let go. I can't lose it."

XIII

I feel great remorse for how I handled cutting out Lucas. In an effort to realign my integrity and return to my spirituality, I spend a sizable sum on a weekend retreat for the Ignatian Spiritual Exercises. The retreat intends to help attendees hear God's call, to begin identifying their vocation through aligning their desires with what is "good." The flip side of this means also understanding the temptation of what Catholics call "the evil one." It is a practice in discerning the good from the bad.

The women in attendance are all mothers except one who has independently consecrated herself to Jesus. She glows with a joy I've rarely seen. Her hair is long and gray, but her face looks like a young child's in its taut softness. She wears modest floral dresses and observes the retreat's commitment to silence when others break it. When I see her I wonder if maybe I want to be like her; maybe I want to consecrate myself to God too. Later in the retreat she says she imagines holding baby Jesus and it brings her to tears. I decide I am not fit for the gig.

On the second day, the priest leads us through a guided meditation where we will allegedly uncover core wounds that left cracks in us, which evil takes advantage of to separate us from love, God. I decide to fully embrace this experience, despite so much of it feeling, frankly, corny. I scrawl in the corner of my notebook, *I am so not Catholic, what am I doing here?* I figure the amount of money I spent, and this being a religious tradition of more years than I can imagine, means I ought to suspend my disbelief, have a bit of humility, and at least give it a real try.

We close our eyes. Eventually, he tells us to identify a painful feeling has been weighing on us lately. Mine are manifold: shame, regret, tunnel-vision lust, exploitation, degradation, loneliness. Then, he instructs us to go back in our memory to the first time in our life we felt this way.

The glow of a screen on ghost white skin of a 12-year-old girl at 1am, addicted to hope her hero might wake up with the sunrise in his eyes and love her.

Now go further back—is there a time even earlier than that?

The moment he says "earlier" I am immediately dropped back into a vivid, rarely accessed memory. The last time I had recalled it, I confided it in my boyfriend through embarrassed laughter. He responded *Molly, there is nothing funny about this. That was not ok. That's the result of neglect.* A prideful bubble burst inside me. Something collapsed; I had held this memory unconsciously in high esteem, some unintegrated young part of me believing it was evidence of my laudable precociousness, my independence and intuitive empowered sexuality. I immediately broke down into tears and snapped at him, saying I didn't want his pity. I didn't want to go there. I shoved it away and reflected no further.

Now, I am confronted with the memory again. It is vivid, and the recollection is ice cold in my core. I had discovered porn recently. I looked at it whenever I had the chance to be alone, which was rare. I instinctively knew it was something I should not tell anyone about. It would be a secret with myself. Somewhere along the way, perhaps through an advertisement, I had discovered a sex chat room.

This night I had an idea. I tiptoed to the computer and logged onto the chat. I had always been a quick learner of vocabulary and had a mind for marketing. Once I emailed the marketing department of Puffs tissue company with a slogan idea: *Noses get picky when they get icky, so pick Puffs!* Tonight's witty turn of phrase on the chat room I created was not so sweet, something no 9-year-old should know how to do. I pointed my webcam down. Messages from strangers poured in. *I bet that feels good, doesn't it?*

No, I did not feel good. I looked at myself on the screen and felt something new. It was not pleasure. It was dizziness and fear. I felt stolen away, foreign, distant, confused, and unbearably alone.

I quickly closed the window and went back to bed, afraid.

These men, these disgusting men, they saw my age in the title, and they looked. Molly, there is nothing funny about this. This was not ok. That's the result of neglect.

This is a time you took a vow to engage in sin, to cope with this core wound. Whatever happened to you was not your fault. Let yourself feel this fully now, and let God's light in to heal it.

Afterwards, the priest walks over to me. He crouches down next to where I'm sitting. He does this to no one but me. He whispers, *Are you going to be alright? Do you need anything?*

I wipe the river of tears from my red cheeks, deepen my stifled breathing, flash a smile and assure him I am fine. I have never felt so abandoned, so hurt, so filled with grief by how unprotected I was. Yet, in my confrontation with this immeasurable wound, I have never felt so much love. I have never felt so close to God.

XIV

In August, I set out on my travels to Ireland to be changed. I hoped to feel moved to write a memoir, to answer the question that emerged from the writing I did at Lucas' urging in May: *Who was I before the internet?* I thought my relationship with him might be a clue. I did not anticipate the clue would be an initiation, an excruciating confrontation with the most soul-crushing malady the internet gave me: an escape into a daydream spurred by a man who could not love me, unboundaried sexual exhibitionism to numb the lonely boredom of invisibility.

As I had before, I did not want to confront what I was running from that this preoccupation concealed. Beneath it all is a deep wound of not being seen, of speaking to an uninterested audience and a piercing silence in return for my eagerness to simply love. I could not bear the empty hours of my youth then or even now as he thrust me back into that dark room I should've stayed out of, that was only ever lit by a pixelated illusion of human touch. I was launched into an autopilot reenactment that my willpower could not break me out of.

In a way, with Lucas, I found the connection I had spent my adolescence fixated on. With a twisted stomach and a hollowness in my chest, I'd stare into a glowing screen, hoping this man in some distant country might still be awake at his 4am long enough for me to read his green font in our chat window, accepting a video chat request. This was so like that, with lust and admiration reciprocated. I found what I wanted. If I look at it from a certain angle, I see I lived a dream through this man. And what became of it? More emptiness, more longing that videos and voice messages could never sate.

XV

I spent months moving on from Lucas. I wrote about his influence and my infatuation in my memoir about traveling to Ireland. We reconnected in a new year, both of us single. Much to my dismay, my feelings of yearning returned. So did our lust for one another. I lost hours to daydreams. After more risqué exchanges, I confessed my openness to trying love down the line at a different stage, if we crossed paths and timing aligned. I considered again what I had desperately tried and failed to ignore the previous year: Maybe this unfolding storyline of my life, maybe it really could be building up to *us*.

I feel like I have two choices: the bad one, to entertain this to satisfy myself, or the good one, to be honest and risk upsetting you. As much as I enjoy our friendship, I personally don't see more happening.

He did it. He told me the truth, the whole truth, no ambiguity. He doesn't want me, never will, he would only ever want photos, voice messages, euphemisms, and my adoration. Thank God, the brutal honesty I need to lift this spell. No more room to doubt, no more room to hope. Clarity.

It settles into my body. I have been 12 years old for another year. I was willing to devote myself to him. I persisted despite his ambivalence. I flattered him despite his mediocrity. I have been 9 years old in my destruction. I told him I don't send photos, and then two weeks later I set up my camera and recorded for him. I delete our chats. I delete every piece of writing I've done for him. I had offered to mail him a card. I find it and rip it apart. I tear up the writing in my journals about him. I rip apart a print I bought by the artist he loves. It is beautiful art, but I cannot look at it.

I pulled tarot cards about us last May. Seven of Swords through January, followed by Strength beginning now through this upcoming May. The Lovers for advice the whole year long, contrasted with Nine of Swords as what I should not do. I pulled tarot last week to try and find the clarity that only tonight, his certain refusal of my whole being, could provide. I don't remember them. Why? It feels like a violation, something spoiled. Why do I give any significance to these cardboard cards? Why do I need to see ahead of me? Why do I need to know? Why am I so willful? I cling to what? This man? Why does my mind spiral around him with such gravity? Why do I feel so desperate for this frankly unexceptional, demonstrably disinterested man to want me? What would his love, his wanting, amount to? I feel so ashamed to be 29 and a lonely child.

The salt on my face hardens like armor, securing me into a conviction I can no longer evade. I stand up and walk with determination towards the garage. I crouch down to the bottom shelf of a cabinet and retrieve a log for a fire. I drop it forcefully into the fireplace and ignite a flame. I collect the shreds of the card, the art, my writing and grab my three tarot decks and their guidebooks. I spend half an hour placing everything on the fire, sitting as close to the flames as I can. I watch it all burn, everything, it's done. I'm done. I'm done with him and anyone like him, before this, after this. I'm done with my daydreaming. I'm done with these attempts to play God, to write the story of my own life like I have any control or insight into other people. I am done with this clinging, my grandiose yearning projected onto anything but heaven, the flimsy cope for a neglect deeper than I can bandage with imaginative escape.

I honestly hope you're doing alright Mole.

He reflects back to me all the good I'm doing, the growth and changes. I wish I could sustain contempt for him, I wish I could commit to a belief in his inferiority, but right now I feel a bitter, embarrassed gratitude. I wish he did not show me such tenderness as he suffocated my foolish hope's last breath. I wish he was not so gentle as he one last time held up the mirror he had for the last nine months. I tried to look past it into him rather than into the reflection of my arrested mind, my fractured spirit. I see it all now, unable to look away. I wish he was not doing what I most desire from love: making the choice to will the good of the other, me, rather than satisfying the will of his self.

I got what I wanted from him after all, didn't I? This rejection was his love.

XVI

God, I fell in love with my daydreams again. The water from the shower head is beating down on my face and my breasts for the second time today. I've been in here for nearly an hour. I fell in love, God. I am pleading with you to never again let me fall in love with my imagination. Why can't I commit to you? You are easy to love but so hard not to stray from. There is a knife in my chest and this wet pressure is digging and twisting and my blood is spiraling down the drain. I haven't had a regular heartbeat in twelve hours.

I know it wasn't truly love I fell into, but despair. My photos and my messages were all the same as before. I am a 9-year-old child, a 12-year-old girl before you, shrinking and powerless. Those arms around me, the chest I nuzzled my tearful face into, they were always yours, weren't they? You held me through it all, not him. Your love, not his. Any love he gave me was yours flowing through his fingertips into my vision, wasn't it? I wish I had it now, but he is not here, nor are you, I fear.

The steam is sedating and I wish I could sleep. If I could just sink into semi-consciousness and wake to ice cold pounding on my skin, maybe I would find stability again. I recall that people cope with pain through self-mutilation, glancing at my razor. I have no urge, never have, save once while being stalked. Truthfully I don't want to hurt more than this. The theater of my own pain is sufficient to express my anguish, the anguish of falling in love with anything but you, God, you. I wish I hadn't needed this, all of it, this fixation and fall. I wish I could've stayed content to long, only to long, not to seek. I sought you out in these men, their selfishness, mine too.

At the retreat the priest told us to go into prayer and ask *What is God's name for you?* Others heard some variation of *my beloved daughter* but all I heard was *divine spark, a catalyst.* I took it merely as evidence of my compensatory grandiosity. If this is truly what you call me, please save me from myself so I might spark change in anyone else. I don't know who I am anymore, lost in men and dreams, fearful hope, consuming lust. I want to find myself through you, only you. If I vowed myself to the lonely escape hatch of compulsion I want to vow myself now to your love. Release me from whatever distraction has seized my wounded heart, my aching womb. I am empty and I need you to fill me again.

I notice a pumice stone hanging off the shelf and try softening my heels. It is too worn down to make a difference. I stay rough. My body yearns to feel someone's skin against mine like the force of this water. I wish I could call the only man who ever truly loved me, who I left in hopes of finding you and finding someone to share in you with. This virtual dream could never love me back.

What if I lost the one you sent me after all? What if in my corruption I gave him up? It's over, God, I lost. I lost him, I lost the plot, I lost the vision, and what if I've lost you too? This is the consequence of my betrayal. I hope it is true that you are forgiving and when I'm ready you'll return.

The droplets on the wall run into each other and it looks like conception, each one created and creating again and again. My fertility is diminishing. I roll over and the water beats on my shoulder. I wonder if I'm sentenced to a life half-awake, half-asleep in my narcissism. I am awake today, rubbing my forefinger against the caulk in the crevice of my shower and wondering what it would feel like on my tongue. The homonym, his girth, the wet shine of desire on pink skin I wished I could taste. I cover my face in humiliation on this private stage, the floor of my piping hot shower turning my body red, that I ever imagined such vacant lust might be a path to love like what you alone can give me. This is a portrait of my nakedness for only you, God. My body, my heartbreak and my regret. Sobriety, steam in my lungs and shame in my gut.

I am foolish to love so quickly. I am a wounded child to imagine his hungry gaze, his sparse words, his superficial flattery could bandage the ache of being unseen, unwanted, and so far from your hand. He fertilized my imagination with the command of a sunset, the full gestation that is bearing my future through words for you. You, God, it's all for you. The knife through my heart theirs, the stabbing force was mine, but the blood seeping out is for you now, your blood was for me, this must be a covenant.

I stand up and grab my razor. I lift my leg up and press my foot against the wall. I run the blade up the full length of my leg and I am smooth again, soft to touch, out of reach of any palm that would want to feel it. If only you could touch me, God, I just want you to touch me. If only I could taste you, God, I just want to taste you.

Molly Frances is a creative nonfiction writer who yearns for God and love. She also dabbles in social commentary from a leftist lens influenced by Catholicism. Her previous work includes the political zine *Floating* and a collaborative zine for people with bipolar disorder, *Euthymia*. She is currently writing a book-length memoir about traveling through Ireland and Belgium on a spiritual pilgrimage, and the transformative power of friendship and heartbreak.

Molly publishes essays on her two Substacks and unfortunately posts frequently on Instagram. Her zines can be purchased on her online shop.

Social commentary: mollyfrances.substack.com

Catholic explorations: holymoley.substack.com

Instagram: @molefrances

Shop (URL): mollyis.online